Praise for Over Easy

T0027078

Ms. Ivans' poems are windows into our lives: the memories, struggles, and simple joys that form our humanity. You will find yourself here.

— Pamela Sheldrick, owner
Pandora Book Peddlers, Madison, NJ

This is a writer who takes her readers on a journey in each poem. Marcia Ivans travels back and forth embracing emotion like a roaring lioness unafraid to tell it like it is. There is no holding back, no questioning as to what to include, no misunderstanding. From the first page, the writer treats us to the truth. Written with gusto, Marcia's poems invite us inside the darkness and the light of a life questioned until peace reigns supreme. *Over Easy* is a gift from the heart.

— Julie Maloney, Director
WOMEN READING ALOUD, Mendham, NJ

Marcia Ivans' *Over Easy* is the candid journey of an intrepid woman who pulled herself out of sadness and into joy, her journal ever at her side. She walks us through the tough times with straightforward punches of language and the confident assurance of one who has beaten the odds and emerged victorious, softball mitt in hand.

— Karen Haefelein, author of *Somehow Romantic*
retired creative writing teacher,
Academy of Visual and Performing Arts,
Red Bank Regional High School, Little Silver, NJ

- Ms. Ivans puts many universal feelings into words. I was touched intimately and profoundly. She says things I am thinking but unable to express. All her work is interesting and much of it speaks to me directly. Brava.

  — Nancy Holland, Ph.D.

- Beginning with reminiscences from childhood times, in *Over Easy*, the reader walks with Ivans through difficult relationships, the deaths of dear friends, on to personal growth and acceptance, and ends by sharing lighthearted humor about everyday situations. Her honesty and wit ring true. I silently wept and laughed out loud. Life has certainly turned Over for Ivans and has become Easy.

  — Rosemary S. McGee, owner, Arseya Publishing, NJ; author of *Spilling My Guts*

- The writer reaches deep into her soul to understand and share her journey. Her honesty in both her sadness and her joy may well inspire the reader to take similar chances.

  — Nancy Cunningham, M.S.W.

Over Easy

poems

MARCIA S. IVANS

ARSEYA PUBLISHING • New Jersey

Library of Congress Control Number: 2007937783

ISBN-13   978-0-9745185-7-2

Design by Curtis Tow Graphics, New York, NY

Author Photo by Jim Somers
Printed in the United States by The Wall Street Group, Inc.

Published by Arseya Publishing
New Vernon, New Jersey
www.arseya.com

FIRST EDITION

Dedicated

With heartfelt love and thanks to

My dear children, Paul, Wendy, and Lynn
who have shared my journey

Jodi, who brought me out of the darkness
into this beautiful light

Rosemary, my friend, my shoulder, my rock

All the women writers along my path
who encouraged and nurtured me

Table of Contents

Past Perfect

Reflections

Your immaculate starched white pinafore
Sparkles through the glass
Golden braids sit atop your head
Your blue eyes glisten with happiness
A smile so real on your cherubic face
Adorable five year old girl
Picture perfect in that old jeweled frame
I know who you are little girl
You are me.

Why don't I remember?

Pink

I remember the stairs that took me to
My land of imagination
Wearing clothes from trunks and taped boxes
I would fly away to anywhere
And be anyone I wanted to be
From that attic of treasures
I escaped to my land of make believe.

In reality, my pink bedroom
Was more my mother than me
Pink skirt on vanity
Walls
Bed covers
Pink and frilly.

Baseball, cops and robbers, cowboys and Indians
That was who I was
Not pink.
Dolls are for girls
She always said.
I thought
Born too soon.

Keepsake

To my dear daughter
I leave you this special glass bottle
Which sits silently on the shelf
So simple, yet so multifaceted
Perhaps you will see me in it as a child playing
And longing for the same life you wanted as a child
Perhaps it will tell what caused our differences
And how, today, we have come together in spite of them
Perhaps you will see the glistening of a teardrop
Or feel the same glow I felt when looking at it
As you are doing now
Remember your great-grandmother
Remember your grandmother
And remember your mother
Know that their lives are encased in this bottle
As yours will be someday.

Drifting Mind

Just before the pleasure of sleep
I recede into my childhood and think
Of totally disconnected scenarios
Which are neither traumatic nor significant.

I remember the Good Humor truck
With its kaleidoscope music
Grey haired Tom telling endless jokes
He was the Pied Piper of Beverly Crest.

I remember the Duncan Yo Yo man at
The local candy store each spring
Teaching us kids new tricks with his
Magical Yo Yo.

I remember riding my red bike
With my brother on his blue bike
Every Sunday morning to the bakery
To buy fresh rolls for breakfast
And a cookie of our choosing as our treat.

I remember when my bedroom window
Was open in the summer to let in the cool breezes
Hearing the roaring crescendos of the crowds
At the local racetrack as each race progressed.

I remember sledding down a hill at
The reservoir after the first good snowfall
Of the season
All of us sneaking through the gate
Which was kindly left open.

I remember playing stickball with the boys
Always being picked last because I was the only girl
Our bats were shortened broom sticks
Our bases were chalk lines on the street.

I remember coming home from school one day
To find a frisky dog being bathed by
Mother in the kitchen sink
Whitey would always sneak out the front door
And run away, choosing not to hear his name called
By my father
He always came back except the night
He didn't hear the trolley car.

As I lie here in bed
I don't remember growing older
I just remember those small vignettes
That shaped my life.

The Stuff of My Life

Bags pushed behind some old shoes

Boxes laying side by side under the bed

Dusty trunks in the attic

Old suitcases in the basement

All contain memories of my past

Pictures in frames and out of frames

Is that really me?

The yearbooks signed by best friends

With nicknames I vaguely remember

A bowling trophy, a jogging trophy

A flower pressed between pages of a scrapbook

Containing a life I once knew

And every few years more items get thrown away

Now all things from the boxes and bags and suitcases

Fit into a small container and in a few years

When I am gone, they will be gone.

A life of stuff.

Pipe Dreams

Deep Inside

Like water freely flowing down a mountain
Through the rocks and then sliding smoothly
Over the paths created by time,
My words find their place
On the paper I use to express those thoughts
Constantly resounding in the silence of my mind.

It is so easy to acknowledge the various
Ups and downs of my emotional self
I long for the ability to express the ebb and flow
Of these thoughts as I hear so many around me do
It would be so freeing to allow myself to speak aloud
What my heart lets me write.

No Doubt

Without a doubt

You are confusing me

Without a doubt

I don't know who I am

Without a doubt

Since I first met you

I'm so sure I don't know anything

Going my own way

Doing my own thing

Bothering no one

Life was so calm.

Expectation

How can I expect you to hear my heart beating
When you enter the room?
How can I expect you to sense the twinge of jealousy
I feel when you give someone else a hug?
How can I expect you to know how I long
To spend a lifetime with you
Not just get by with scattered moments?
How can I expect you to know
I want to raise you up to view the beauty of life
When your heart is down?
How can I expect you to see that in my eyes
You are wonderful just as you are?
How can I expect you to guess that when we are
Sitting so close together
Almost touching
I pray for an embrace
But know that you will not?
How can I expect you to know?
Because

I am telling you now.

Let Go

Soar with me to that unused place

Of forgotten feelings

Those wonderful sensations of

Caring, laughter and love.

Let us both release the fear of being hurt

The fear of broken promises

I want to feel the giddiness of my youth again

With you.

The Performance

The excitement of seeing
A massive display of fireworks
Against a blackened sky
Is akin to the explosion
We lovers create at the
Height of emotion.
After the performance
The reflective silence of the sky
Evokes a peaceful calm in
Our hearts and breaths.

Don't

You can mess with my heart

You can mess with my soul

You can mess with my mind

But don't mess with my hair!

Rubber Bands

Rubber bands pulled taut

Extreme emotions from within

My reactions to you

Allowed your moods to control me

Give up

Let go

Get away

Intellectually, I know it

They know it too

This is the truth.

Time runs too swiftly

Not much remaining

Alone too long

Cannot tolerate much more

Choice is difficult.

Mirrors

I look at you and see myself
I hear your angry, jealous words
That for years were my own.

I see you as I was
Afraid to care
Because of past hurts.

Time has shown me many levels of friendships
But, I also need one special person
To share intimate and deep feelings.

I have learned that small talk is
Sharing life's experiences
Not wasted words that
You see as unimportant.

I remember the years I felt tight and tense
My mind and body engulfed by fear of
Being hurt
When I would not allow myself to feel free
And let some happiness and laughter in.

No one could release the negatives
I alone needed to let go
And relieve my own sadness.

My selfishness needed to push you
To be who I wanted you to be
I deeply regret that.
I thought I was helping
Apparently not.

Pipe Dreams

Salty water runs down my cheeks
Hopes fading into lost dreams
Drops of sadness wet my heart
Promises of love and trust.

I waited
Years of false beliefs
You lured me with a smile
Me wanting so much
I stayed entwined in your web.

One angry outburst too many
I must walk away now
To hold onto my dignity.

My teardrops fall quietly
Like rain sliding down a window pane.

.Links

Friends and Journals

A warm friend is like a trusted journal
Both hold the stories of our lives inside
Tears cried with our friends
Dot the pages of our journals
As we give fresh flowers to those friends
We entrust the journal with dried petals from lovers.

Silence surrounds our friends as they
Listen to our sorrow and pain
Just as the journal remains silent
Holding the secrets of our sad hearts.

We share laughter and joy with both
One echoes the sounds
The other retains that gladness on its
Pages forever.

Pleasant Passing

White puffy clouds carry her to the place

Of everlasting peace and tranquility

Beautiful, beckoning lights shine

And welcome her

Letting her drift toward the rainbow of colors

All the tension and unrest in her being released

Gone is the pain from the physical and mental

Her soul finally free.

Sitting With Mary

We sit quietly with hands intertwined
My love for you flows through our touching fingertips
We have spent many hours together in this room
With few words spoken.

You slept most of the time,
Awakened only by the sound of your own cough
We had tea to warm us
Then you slept once again.
Eating breakfast together was a happy time
After you ate, we walked back to your favorite couch.

Tucked in and comfortable you looked me in the eye
And said "Lets talk."
We spoke about the beauty of the white light
To be followed to the other side
And all the love that would welcome you
From all those to whom you had given so much of yourself.

Too many subjects to talk about in too short a time.
Then we again clasped first one hand, then intertwined both
And sat quietly and lovingly, both of us knowing.

Time Between Lives

It was at a time when I was ready to give up on life
The arc of darkness crept up on me
My familiar and safe territory.
As the months of heaviness gave way to a small
Glimmer of light
You, my friend, told me you had only six months to live.

Twenty years ago, almost to the day
Another friend talked to me of the same thing
The growth would consume her
Then it would be done
No more pain and suffering
She told me of her wish to die.

You share the same name
I was frightened by the similarities
Knowing that as I was
Clinging to my small ray of hope
You each described your desire to be loved as you died
Giving me the will to want to be there for you
We spoke openly and honestly
With laughter and tears
Until it was time to say goodbye.

Shapes

Circles and squares

Life and death

Friends and enemies

Friends are enemies

Changes and feelings

Changes change feelings

Round and round

The circle has to stop

Let the circle

Become a square

Bring peace.

Links

Were it not for the strength

Of our friendships

Our enemies would not stay weak.

Indecent Exposure

Hidden Feelings

Write the words

Bring them out

From the back

Of your mind

Where they are

Hidden from view

Hidden from sound

Don't dare

Speak them

Or they will become

Reality.

Why.

If you do not question and probe

If you do not seek answers

And search for truths

How do you know you are unhappy?

Churning

Churning, churning, look outside

Yearning, yearning, look inside

I see the good that's in my life.

I have searched for happiness

All these years

Books and lectures and quotes galore

I can recite them word for word.

Each day I pray and give thanks

And ask for the strength

To knock down the walls within

Which keep me from loving myself.

Over Easy

Happiness took a long time.

Darkness, despair, hate, rage, anger, fear,
Insecurity, guilt, self loathing, pain
Descriptions of a life
Which almost ended by my own hand.

You once said the will to live
As little as was contained
In my pinkie toe
Was stronger than all the negatives
Trying to drain the life from me.

For years
I sat in silence
I sat with tears
I fought
I cursed
I yelled
I hated
I clung.
There were times I substituted
My medicine for yours.

That roller coaster life was my safety net
A security blanket
I could not
I would not let go.

I hated those times of deafening silence
While you waited for my words
To surface from the abyss of my being.

Rising slowly to where I am today
One step forward
Two steps back.
Those years were an eternity.

Two as One

I am of one body
But two different people therein
Whose lives are totally separate
Open me to my core and see rays of sunshine
From that woman who has recovered from
Much pain and sadness
Happy, proud of her progress
Her accomplishments
Cared for by some, liked by some, admired by some
Intimately loved by no one
She survives.

The dark side resides
Under heavy clouds of anger and loneliness
Always ready to strike
Like an addiction of sorts
Lurid and black, lustful and negative
Consumed by hurtful thoughts to others
But mostly herself
Comfortably familiar old behavior
She hears words of reproach
Laughs inside, knowing
She will not stop her destructive thoughts
On the outside, her rage will explode
Spewing from her inner darkness
And sends that other part of her
To the depths of despair.

Feeling unloved is akin to having
A rock tied around her neck
Which hangs heavier every day.

Illusions

I was the stem supporting the large
Brilliantly colored peony
The many petals clung to me
In this way, we gave one another strength and beauty.
But as the frigid winter journey began
The fierce winds of change whipped around
And the beauty I believed would always be part of me
Drifted away.
Many times during the darkness
I envisioned new growth
Almost allowing myself to feel it
And grasp it
Only to discover it was just an illusion.
The harshness of the storm
Revealed my deep torment, twisted obsessions
Avoidance of truths, self loathing and deep pain
A barren and bent twig deliberately crushing
Myself into my own emptiness.

Temptation

Today, I feel your power
Luring me with the strength of the devil
Back to memories of fun times,
Carefree days and party nights
Sparkled knowing you would be there
To give me courage when I felt weak
Bolster the lost soul
Hiding deep inside
To new heights of confidence.

Fear blows over me like a cold wind
I shiver and shake as I reach to call
No answer, no answer, no answer
Cell phones, home phones, pagers
No help at all today.

I run to a place I pray she will be
My shoulder, my strength, my rock.
Not many questions, only quiet comfort.

The tears come
Your grip loosens its hold
You fade away laughing
Knowing you can return
Any time you wish.

Storms of the Heart

I walk up the stairs to the celebration
Hear the sounds of laughter
Smell the aroma of beer and wine
Watch embraces filled with love
Warmth overflows this room
Not my family
Hers
Glad you learned from them my son.

My heart rumbles as the sky before a storm
My eyes tear like mist in the air
Envy rips my mind
Shatters bones, crushes gains
Ever craving love and affection
From family too distant in miles and emotion.

Ladder climbed ever so slowly
From emptiness and despair
To feeling joyous love.

Today, one rung breaks
I cry
Tomorrow's sun dries the tears.

Rebirth

Just Once

Just once I would like to hear you say
"I am happy for you" without a but

Just once I would like you to believe me
when I tell you my feelings are real

Just once I would like to leave you
in the same happy state of mind
that I walked in with

Just once I would like to walk out
without being angry at you
for not understanding me

Just once I would like to go and
not feel such rage that I want to hurt you
with spiteful words

Just once I want to be right about
what I tell you concerning
deep secret feelings

Just once I would like to be
totally honest
and not deny the truth.

Waiting

The ticking of the small clock
Shatters the silence of the room
Thunder roars through my brain
Disturbing the fragile state of being
I have chosen.

A safe place to float and avoid life
My comfort zone
Neither happy nor sad
Afraid to break through the barrier
I built so long ago.

My created jail of self-loathing
Must be smashed now
Push through it, run through it
Grab those loving hands
Reaching to guide me.

Dear Power of the Universe
Give me the strength to release the past
And take the first step toward freedom.

Rebirth

Ascending out of the darkness

Swaying with the soft breezes

Inhaling the fragrance of the rose

Tasting the cool droplets floating from the sky

Savoring life's beauty around me

Feeling the love of friends heals my heart

Accepting the love of a love feels divine

Floating on the softness of discovery

Hopelessness and despair had smothered me

The sadness feels like it lasted a lifetime

Perhaps it did.

Yellow Forsythia

Lying dormant for too long

Rising from the hard cold earth

Daring winter to make its exit

Bringing light from darkness

Stretching my branches

Feeling the warmth of the sun

Growing and alive again

I am yellow forsythia.

Bubbles

Moments of happiness
Wrapped in bubbles of glass
They would burst
Always did
Nothing ever lasted for this heart.

All my life
Brief glimmers of light
Then the crash
Inside my head
The shards slamming me
Back to blackness.

Fast forward
One good month
Six good months
A little shaky now and then
One good year
Keep it going
Another day
It's okay
Another day
I'm okay
Let the bubbles explode
Carrying my old fears away.

The Small Smile

From beyond your usually stoic face

A smile curls onto your lips

The glimmer of satisfaction

At the serenity I have found

After many years of revealing myself

To finally reach the discovery of my truth

And be able to smile too.

Not Bad At All

It's not too bad to feel good

It doesn't hurt too much

To look into the mirror and like what I see

It's not much harder to be

Happy than be sad

In fact, it's easier to smile than to frown

Not worrying is more fun than fretting

Being nice to others

Feels better than being curt and angry

Rather than being concerned

With what I think I am unable to do

I concentrate on all that I love to do

It's too bad it took me so long to discover

That it's easier to feel good than be unhappy

I won't waste any more time

Thinking about it!

The Prize

I am a winner
Not of a blue ribbon to adorn my clothing
Not of a satchel stuffed with money
To spend recklessly
Not of a mansion staffed by beautiful people
Nor even an airplane to fly me to exotic isles.

I have struggled hard and long
I have cried too many tears
I have mended a shattered heart
And endured painful losses.

The treasures I have now are riches
Won by attaining the level of peace
That comes at the end of suffering
Peace I have longed for
All my life.

Skipping Along

Corn

Corn, pure gushy corn
That's what I write about
Simplistic truths are mostly corn
Hearts and flowers with violins
For sure
But I write what I feel
About those simple truths
That have given me the will to live
The same feelings and inspirations
That changed my life
Made it all worthwhile
These same feelings, thoughts and truths
Are there for everyone to have, see and feel
But I was blessed enough
To have been given the chance
To understand how easy it is to enjoy life
There's much to be said about the fact
I've almost eliminated anger from my life
Worry is hardly a part of me anymore
I can feel happiness
Almost every day
Sometimes the secret to enjoying life
Is so simple that we pass it right by.

First

I am not afraid to be first anymore
When talking, that is,
In school I was always first on line
Because I was always the shortest
But I never raised my hand first
To answer a question, that is,
Because I was afraid my reply would be wrong
Even though it was the same
As the person who answered first.

However, now that I pen my own thoughts
On paper, that is,
I do raise my hand to go first
At classes and readings and such, that is
Because these words are written from my heart,
And my heart is always right
Most of the time, that is.

Break a Leg

I am an actress

I am a poet

I ventured into the world of poetry

Almost as good as acting

There were small steps to take

Write, correct, read aloud

Gentle nudges to create more

Gaining confidence slowly

Readings, signings, publishing and sales

Expanding my repertoire

First friends listened

Then family

Other writers heard my words

Now strangers pay attention

The stage is lit.

Smile! It's SHOWTIME!

The Mitt, the Bat and I

The notice in the paper was small
Women's softball league forming
Only two requirements
Must have own mitt
Must be over twenty five
Okay, I'm ready!
Two games a week
I can handle that.

Stretch the unused muscles
Toss the ball around
Oops, missed that one
Bump on chin
That's okay
This is fun.

It was easy to play in the field
I was assigned a position
Where no hits ever reached
Except the one I missed
That's okay
This is fun.

First time at bat
I surely can hit that big ball
Swing, swing, swing
You're out!
That's okay
This is fun.

The family is coming
To cheer Grandma on
I pray to the Power High above
With all of my might
That I may please, please, please
Get a hit tonight.
This is fun.

Wearing my purple team jersey
I stand at the plate
With bat held tight
A swing and a miss
I have one strike
Here comes the ball
My bat held strong
I hit it to my surprise
This is fun.

I race to first base
And hear voices behind me
"Go Grandma, go!"
And stand there with pride
This sixtyish body has survived
An evening of softball.
Oh yes,
This is fun.

Sample This

Requirement necessary for
Part time job
Drink lots of water
Visit lab
I am ready
Nurse is here
Take the cup
Much too small
Blue pill in bowl
Do not run water
Five minutes only
I wait
She waits
Right outside the door
Clock keeps ticking
And I wait
And she waits
The dam is full
Ready to burst
One minute left
Could not do it
On command
Time is up
I failed this test!

Semantics

Some claim I am too needy
Absolutely, undeniably not true.
It's just that I am very wanty
For the simple experiences
Life has to offer
Like laughter, hugs and love.
Wanty for the brightness of days
And the calm of star filled nights
For the friendships of today
And for the release
Of those from yesterday
That are mine no more.
Needy, no!
Wanty, yes!
I like my choice.

Stages of Ages

I am at the stage in life where
I am considered upper-middle-age or
Perhaps, lower-old-age
I am really not sure because
The image in the mirror changes often.
It sometimes reflects my mother's
Worn wrinkly face
I look away then.
Another time I see a young woman
Playing softball
Wait a minute!
That was only yesterday.
I see a mother on skis with her offspring
Then an older woman embracing grandchildren
I see a brave woman going to work
Dressed as Peter Pan
And a thirty year old woman with a clown face
Driving around New York City
Asking for directions to the circus
Embarrassing her son and daughter
Hiding on the floor of the car.

My mirror reflects a face of triumph
As I hold a trophy for Oldest Female Finisher
In a five mile race
That woman reflecting back at me
Doesn't really know her stage or age.
This woman who wears a red hat to restaurants
Writes humorous poems
So different from the words of earlier years
When sadness was her life, says
LOOK AT ME!
I am at exactly the stage and age
Where I want to be.

Skipping Along

We have been dull, basic, and proper
Since she was a child
White only
Polished often
Laces bleached
Sparkling clean.

Now we are rebels
Wild, carefree
Vibrant colors
Dazzling sunset orange
Sparkling rose pink
Brilliant sea blue
Jumping and dancing.

Oh my,
At her age
Wearing sneakers like us!

The Author

Marcia S. Ivans began writing poetry over twenty-five years ago — her first book of poems, *Yesterday: A Collection of Thoughts* was published in 1981 and reissued in 2003. As her writing gathered momentum, she found herself sharing both her written words and the healing process of creating them with audiences around New Jersey. Marcia is a member of Women Who Write, Inc. of Morris County, and has served on its governing board for two years. She began hosting Poetry and Pastries, in 2004, a bimonthly open poetry reading at Café Beethoven in Chatham, NJ. Marcia was a guest reader at the William Paterson University — Victor Talerico Poetry Contest Awards Night in both 2005 and 2007. Her poems have appeared in various newspapers and anthologies: Compassionate Friends of Morris Area Chapter Newsletter; the Morris County Recorder Newspaper; Goldfinch, the Literary Magazine of Women Who Write; the Daily Record of Morris County; and the Poet's Corner section of the Chatham Courier. Marcia lives in Morris County, New Jersey.